Guitar

Scales, Arpeggios & Studies

for Trinity College London Guitar
& Plectrum Guitar exams
from 2016

Initial–Grade 5

Published by
Trinity College London
www.trinitycollege.com

Registered in England
Company no. 02683033
Charity no. 1014792

Printed in England by Caligraving Ltd.

Guitar Initial

Candidates to prepare i) Technical exercise
Technical exercise in C major (music may be used, ♩ = 80)

Candidates to prepare in full *either* section ii) *or* section iii)

either ii) Scales & arpeggios (from memory, *mf*)
Candidates should prepare scales and arpeggios as listed below.
When the examiner requests a key, the candidate should play the scale and then the arpeggio.

G major A minor	to 5th	*im* fingering	scales: *apoyando* or *tirando* (candidate's choice) arpeggios: *tirando*	min. tempi: scales: ♩ = 80 arpeggios: ♩ = 100

or iii) Studies (music may be used)

Candidates to prepare 1a *or* 1b; 2a *or* 2b; and 3a *or* 3b (three studies in total).

The candidate will choose one study to play first; the examiner will then select one of the remaining two prepared studies to be performed.

1a. Star Gazer	or	1b. Playground Games	for tone and phrasing
2a. Submarine	or	2b. Stop It!	for articulation
3a. Ice Breaker	or	3b. Cross String Thing	for idiomatic elements

i) Technical exercise

In C major

ii) Scales & arpeggios

G major scale (to 5th), *apoyando* or *tirando*

G major arpeggio (to 5th), *tirando*

Initial continued

A minor scale (to 5th), *apoyando* or *tirando*

A minor arpeggio (to 5th), *tirando*

iii) Studies

1a. Star Gazer – tone and phrasing (legato)

1b. Playground Games – tone and phrasing (legato)

2a. Submarine – articulation (tirando thumb articulation)

2b. Stop It! – articulation (right finger string damping)

3a. Ice Breaker – idiomatic elements (strummed open chords and tirando)

3b. Cross String Thing – idiomatic elements (tirando)

Guitar Grade 1

Candidates to prepare i) Technical exercise				
Technical exercise in G major (music may be used, ♩ = 56)				
Candidates to prepare in full *either* section ii) *or* section iii)				
***either* ii) Scales & arpeggios** (from memory, *mf*) Candidates should prepare scales and arpeggios as listed below. When the examiner requests a key, the candidate should play the scale and then the arpeggio.				
C major F major	scales: one octave arpeggios: to 5th	*im* fingering	scales: *apoyando* or *tirando* (candidate's choice) arpeggios: *tirando*	min. tempi: scales: ♩ = 56 arpeggios: ♩ = 112
E natural minor		scale: *p* fingering arpeggio: *pim* fingering	*tirando*	
***or* iii) Studies** (music may be used)				
Candidates to prepare 1a *or* 1b; 2a *or* 2b; and 3a *or* 3b (three studies in total). The candidate will choose one study to play first; the examiner will then select one of the remaining two prepared studies to be performed.				
1a. Paper Tiger	*or*	1b. Highland Memories	for tone and phrasing	
2a. Scary Monsters	*or*	2b. Rock Bottom	for articulation	
3a. Poisson Rouge	*or*	3b. Firefly Sky	for idiomatic elements	

i) Technical exercise

In G major

ii) Scales & arpeggios

C major scale (one octave), *apoyando* or *tirando*

C major arpeggio (to 5th), *tirando*

F major scale (one octave), *apoyando* or *tirando*

F major arpeggio (to 5th), *tirando*

E natural minor scale (one octave), *tirando*

E minor arpeggio (to 5th), *tirando*

l.v. (let ring)

iii) Studies

1a. Paper Tiger – tone and phrasing (crescendo and diminuendo)

1b. Highland Memories – tone and phrasing (even tone and bass over-ringing)

Grade 1 continued

2a. Scary Monsters – articulation (staccato)

2b. Rock Bottom – articulation (right hand staccato and tirando thumb strokes)

3a. Poisson Rouge – idiomatic elements (tirando)

3b. Firefly Sky – idiomatic elements (natural harmonics)

Guitar Grade 2

Candidates to prepare i) Technical exercise				
Technical exercise in D major (music may be used, ♩ = 86)				

Candidates to prepare in full either section ii) or section iii)				
either **ii) Scales & arpeggios** (from memory, *mf*) Candidates should prepare scales and arpeggios as listed below. When the examiner requests a key, the candidate should play the scale and then the arpeggio.				
F major	one octave	*p* fingering	scale and arpeggio: *tirando*	min. tempi: scales: ♩ = 62 arpeggios: ♩ = 94
D melodic minor A harmonic minor		*im* fingering	scales: *apoyando* or *tirando* (candidate's choice) arpeggios: *tirando*	
Chromatic scale starting on G		*im* fingering	*apoyando* or *tirando* (candidate's choice)	min. ♩ = 94
or **iii) Studies** (music may be used)				
Candidates to prepare 1a *or* 1b; 2a *or* 2b; and 3a *or* 3b (three studies in total).				
The candidate will choose one study to play first; the examiner will then select one of the remaining two prepared studies to be performed.				
1a. Skater's Waltz	*or*	1b. Linecraft	for tone and phrasing	
2a. Tin Drum	*or*	2b. Porcupine Stomp	for articulation	
3a. Lost and Found	*or*	3b. Mystic Drummer	for idiomatic elements	

i) Technical exercise

In D major

ii) Scales & arpeggios

F major scale (one octave), *tirando*

F major arpeggio (one octave), *tirando*

Grade 2 continued

D melodic minor scale (one octave), *apoyando* or *tirando*

D minor arpeggio (one octave), *tirando*

A harmonic minor scale (one octave), *apoyando* or *tirando*

A minor arpeggio (one octave), *tirando*

Chromatic scale starting on G (one octave), *apoyando* or *tirando*

iii) Studies

1a. Skater's Waltz – tone and phrasing (crescendo and diminuendo)

1b. Linecraft – tone and phrasing (dynamics and two-part balance)

2a. Tin Drum – articulation (accents)

Grade 2 continued

2b. Porcupine Stomp – articulation (left hand staccato)

3a. Lost and Found – idiomatic elements (two-note chords)

3b. Mystic Drummer – idiomatic elements (tambora)

Guitar Grade 3

Candidates to prepare i) Technical exercise

Technical exercise in G major (music may be used, ♩. = 56)

Candidates to prepare in full *either* section ii) *or* section iii)

either ii) **Scales & arpeggios** (from memory, *mf*)

Candidates should prepare scales and arpeggios as listed below.

When the examiner requests a key, the candidate should play the scale and then the arpeggio.

C major A major B natural minor E harmonic minor	two octaves	scales: *im* and *ma* arpeggios: *pppimim*	scales: *apoyando* or *tirando* (candidate's choice) arpeggios: *tirando*	min. tempi: scales: ♩ = 70 arpeggios: ♩. = 38
C major scale in thirds	one octave	*im*	*tirando*	

or iii) **Studies** (music may be used)

Candidates to prepare 1a *or* 1b; 2a *or* 2b; and 3a *or* 3b (three studies in total).

The candidate will choose one study to play first; the examiner will then select one of the remaining two prepared studies to be performed.

1a. It Could be Sweet	*or*	1b. The Tone Zone	for tone and phrasing
2a. Sunflower	*or*	2b. Finger Pickin' Good	for articulation
3a. On Brooklyn Bridge	*or*	3b. Half Way There	for idiomatic elements

i) Technical exercise

In G major

ii) Scales & arpeggios

C major scale (two octaves), *im* and *ma*, *apoyando* or *tirando*

C major arpeggio (two octaves), *tirando*

Grade 3 continued

A major scale (two octaves), *im* and *ma*, *apoyando* or *tirando*

A major arpeggio (two octaves), *tirando*

B natural minor scale (two octaves), *im* and *ma*, *apoyando* or *tirando*

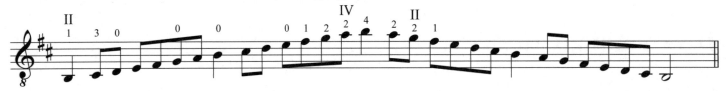

B minor arpeggio (two octaves), *tirando*

E harmonic minor scale (two octaves), *im* and *ma*, *apoyando* or *tirando*

E minor arpeggio (two octaves), *tirando*

C major scale in thirds (one octave), *tirando*

iii) Studies

1a. It Could be Sweet – tone and phrasing (tone colour)

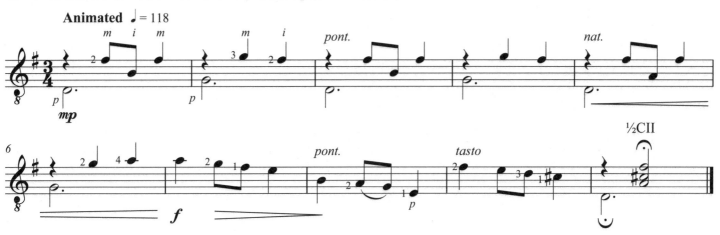

1b. The Tone Zone – tone and phrasing (tone colour)

2a. Sunflower – articulation (ascending slurs)

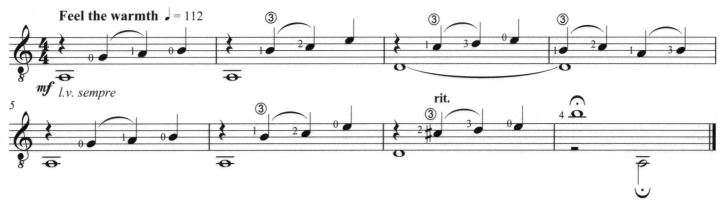

Grade 3 continued

2b. Finger Pickin' Good – articulation (ascending slurs)

3a. On Brooklyn Bridge – idiomatic elements (half barré)

3b. Half Way There – idiomatic elements (half barré)

Guitar Grade 4

Candidates to prepare i) Technical exercise				
Technical exercise in A major (music may be used, ♩ = 130)				
Candidates to prepare in full *either* section ii) *or* section iii)				
either **ii) Scales & arpeggios** (from memory, *mf*) Candidates should prepare scales and arpeggios as listed below. When the examiner requests a key, the candidate should play the scale and then the arpeggio.				
E major Bb major G melodic minor D harmonic minor Chromatic scale starting on F	two octaves	scales: *im* and *ma* arpeggios: *pppima*	scales: *apoyando* or *tirando* (candidate's choice) arpeggios: *tirando*	min. tempi: scales: ♩ = 82 arpeggios: ♩. = 44
Dominant 7th arpeggio in the key of D major		*ppimim...*		min. ♩ = 66
or **iii) Studies** (music may be used)				
Candidates to prepare 1a *or* 1b; 2a *or* 2b; and 3a *or* 3b (three studies in total). The candidate will choose one study to play first; the examiner will then select one of the remaining two prepared studies to be performed.				
1a. Half Moon	*or*	1b. Flamenco Fantasy	for tone and phrasing	
2a. River	*or*	2b. And Relax...	for articulation	
3a. Dark Maze	*or*	3b. Sorrow	for idiomatic elements	

i) Technical exercise

In A major

ii) Scales & arpeggios

E major scale (two octaves), *im* and *ma*, *apoyando* or *tirando*

Grade 4 continued

E major arpeggio (two octaves), *tirando*

Bb major scale (two octaves), *im* and *ma*, *apoyando* or *tirando*

Bb major arpeggio (two octaves), *tirando*

G melodic minor scale (two octaves), *im* and *ma*, *apoyando* or *tirando*

G minor arpeggio (two octaves), *tirando*

D harmonic minor scale (two octaves), *im* and *ma*, *apoyando* or *tirando*

D minor arpeggio (two octaves), *tirando*

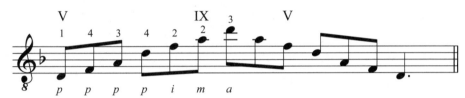

Chromatic scale starting on F (two octaves), *im* and *ma*, *apoyando* or *tirando*

Dominant 7th arpeggio in the key of D major (two octaves), *tirando*

iii) Studies

1a. Half Moon – tone and phrasing (tone colour and dynamics)

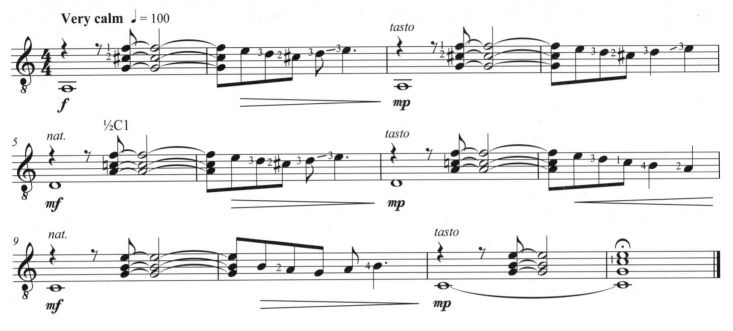

1b. Flamenco Fantasy – tone and phrasing (tone colour and dynamics)

2a. River – articulation (ascending and descending slurs)

2b. And Relax... – articulation (glissando)

Grade 4 continued

3a. Dark Maze – idiomatic elements (chords in 6ths)

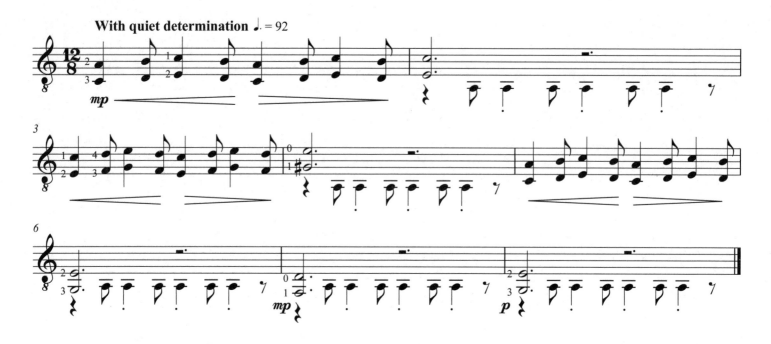

3b. Sorrow – idiomatic elements (three string chords)

Guitar Grade 5

Candidates to prepare i) Technical exercise
Technical exercise in F♯ minor (music may be used, ♩ = 126)

Candidates to prepare in full either section ii) or section iii)

either **ii) Scales & arpeggios** (from memory, *mf*)
Candidates should prepare scales and arpeggios as listed below.
When the examiner requests a key, the candidate should play the scale and then the arpeggio.

E♭ major F major A natural minor C melodic minor	two octaves	scales: *im* and *ma* arpeggios: *ppppima*	scales: *apoyando* or *tirando* (candidate's choice) arpeggios: *tirando*	min. tempi: scales: ♩ = 92 arpeggios: ♩. = 50
G major scale in broken thirds	one octave	*im*	*tirando*	min. ♩ = 82
C major scale in sixths		*ip/mp*		
Dominant 7th arpeggio in the key of A major Diminished 7th arpeggio starting on E	two octaves	*ppimim...*		min. ♩ = 76

or **iii) Studies** (music may be used)

Candidates to prepare 1a *or* 1b; 2a *or* 2b; and 3a *or* 3b (three studies in total).

The candidate will choose one study to play first; the examiner will then select one of the remaining two prepared studies to be performed.

1a. Incognito	*or*	1b. Over the Moon	for tone and phrasing
2a. Mistral	*or*	2b. And So It Ends	for articulation
3a. Mare Nectaris	*or*	3b. All Barre One	for idiomatic elements

i) Technical exercise

In F♯ minor

ii) Scales & arpeggios

E♭ major scale (two octaves), *im* and *ma*, *apoyando* or *tirando*

E♭ major arpeggio (two octaves), *tirando*

F major scale (two octaves), *im* and *ma*, *apoyando* or *tirando*

F major arpeggio (two octaves), *tirando*

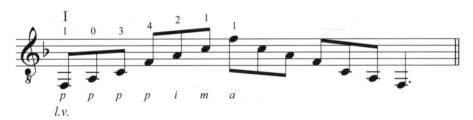

A natural minor scale (two octaves), *im* and *ma*, *apoyando* or *tirando*

A minor arpeggio (two octaves), *tirando*

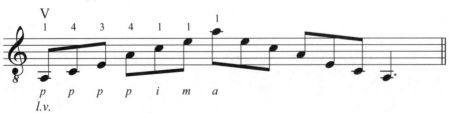

C melodic minor scale (two octaves), *im* and *ma, apoyando* or *tirando*

C minor arpeggio (two octaves), *tirando*

G major scale in broken thirds (one octave), *tirando*

C major scale in sixths (one octave), *tirando*

Dominant 7th arpeggio in the key of A major (two octaves), *tirando*

Grade 5 continued

Diminished 7th arpeggio starting on E (two octaves), *tirando*

iii) Studies

1a. Incognito – tone and phrasing (octaves)

1b. Over the Moon – tone and phrasing (syncopation)

2a. Mistral – articulation (arpeggios)

2b. And So It Ends – articulation (slurring)

Grade 5 continued

3a. Mare Nectaris – idiomatic elements (full barré)

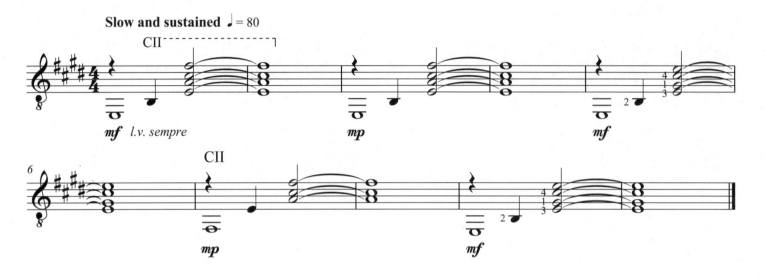

3b. All Barré One – idiomatic elements (full barré)

Plectrum Guitar Initial

Both sections i) *and* ii) to be performed from memory:			
i) Scales: C and G major D minor	min. ♩ = 60	to 5th, ascending and descending	*mf*
ii) Arpeggios: C and G major D minor			

i) Scales

C major scale (to 5th)

G major scale (to 5th)

D minor scale (to 5th)

ii) Arpeggios

C major arpeggio (to 5th)

G major arpeggio (to 5th)

D minor arpeggio (to 5th)

⊓ = Downstroke

V = Upstroke

Plectrum Guitar Grade 1

All sections i) to iii) to be performed from memory:			
i) Scales: C and G major A natural minor	min. ♩ = 72	one octave	*mf*
ii) Arpeggios: C and G major A minor			
iii) Chord sequence: I-V⁷-I in C major			

i) Scales

C major scale (one octave)

G major scale (one octave)

A natural minor scale (one octave)

ii) Arpeggios

C major arpeggio (one octave)

G major arpeggio (one octave)

A minor arpeggio (one octave)

iii) Chord sequence

I-V^7-I in C major

Plectrum Guitar Grade 2

All sections i) to iv) to be performed from memory:			
i) Scales: D major – open D major – closed B♭ major	min. ♩ = 88	one octave	***p* or *f*** as requested by the examiner
E harmonic minor A jazz melodic minor		two octaves	
ii) Arpeggio: D major		one octave	
iii) Broken chords: E minor		two octaves	
A minor		to 12th	
iv) Chord sequences: II-V⁷-I in C major II-V-I in D major			

i) Scales

D major scale – open (one octave)

D major scale – closed (one octave)

B♭ major scale (one octave)

E harmonic minor scale (two octaves)

A jazz melodic minor scale (two octaves)

ii) Arpeggio

D major arpeggio (one octave)

iii) Broken chords

E minor broken chord (two octaves)

A minor broken chord (to 12th)

iv) Chord sequences

II–V⁷–I in C major

II–V–I in D major

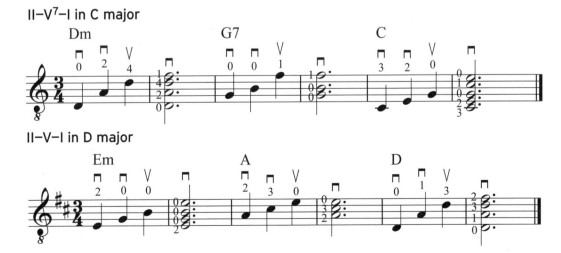

Plectrum Guitar Grade 3

All sections i) to iv) to be performed from memory:			
i) Scales: C and A major B harmonic minor G melodic minor G pentatonic major	min. ♩ = 60	two octaves	***p*** or ***f*** as requested by the examiner
ii) Arpeggio: C major			
iii) Exercises: Bb major – ascending slurs G minor – half barré study			
iv) Chord sequence: II–V⁷–I in G major			

i) Scales

C major scale (two octaves)

A major scale (two octaves)

B harmonic minor scale (two octaves)

G melodic minor scale (two octaves)

G pentatonic major scale (two octaves)

ii) Arpeggio

C major arpeggio (two octaves)

iii) Exercises

B♭ major – ascending slurs

G minor – half barré study

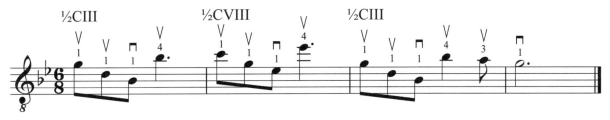

iv) Chord sequence

II–V^7–I in G major

Plectrum Guitar Grade 4

All sections i) to iv) to be performed from memory:			
i) Scales: E major – open E major – closed A natural minor F♯ harmonic minor	min. ♩ = 68	two octaves	*p, mf* or *f* as requested by the examiner
ii) Arpeggio: Dominant 7th in the key of A			
iii) Exercises: F major – IV-V-I D major – slurred F♯ minor – half barré study			
iv) Chord sequence: D major-B⁷-Em⁷-A⁷			

i) Scales

E major scale – open (two octaves)

E major scale – closed (two octaves)

A natural minor scale (two octaves)

F♯ harmonic minor scale (two octaves)

ii) Arpeggio

Dominant 7th arpeggio in the key of A (two octaves)

iii) Exercises

F major – IV–V–I

D major – slurred

F# minor – half barré study

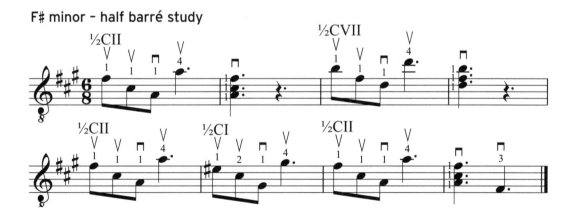

iv) Chord sequence

D major–B⁷–Em⁷–A⁷

D major-B⁷-Em⁷-A⁷

Plectrum Guitar Grade 5

All sections i) to iv) to be performed from memory:			
i) Scales: B major G natural minor F harmonic and melodic minor E dorian	min. ♩ = 80	two octaves	**_p, mf_ or _f_** as requested by the examiner
ii) Arpeggio: Diminished 7th starting and finishing on C			
iii) Exercises: I-VI-II-V⁷-I in G major A major – paired slurs			
iv) Chord sequence: F#m⁷-Bm⁷-Em⁹-A⁷			

i) Scales

B major scale (two octaves)

G natural minor scale (two octaves)

F harmonic minor scale (two octaves)

F melodic minor scale (two octaves)

E dorian scale (two octaves)

ii) Arpeggio

Diminished 7th arpeggio on C (two octaves)

iii) Exercises

I-VI-II-V⁷-I in G major

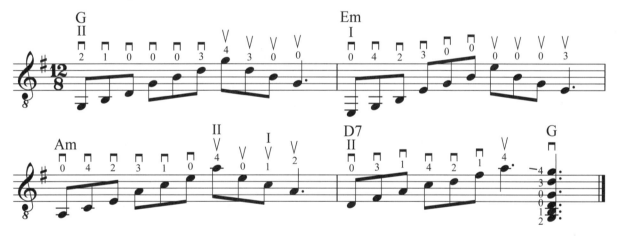

A major – paired slurs

iv) Chord sequence

F#m⁷-Bm⁷-Em⁹-A⁷

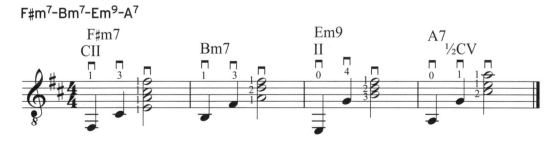